John Hall

Other books by John Hall

Poems
Between the Cities
Days
Meaning Insomnia
Malolactic Ferment
Couch Grass
Repressed Intimations
Else Here: Selected Poems
Couldn't You?
The Week's Bad Groan
Interscriptions (with Peter Hughes)
Keepsache (a companion selection to Else Here)
A Salutation to Poetry (with Emily Critchley)
Later (with Ian Tyson)

Fiction
Apricot Pages

Essays
Thirteen Ways of Talking about Performance Writing
Essays on Performance Writing, Poetics and Poetry
    Volume 1: On Performance Writing,
        with Pedagogical Sketches;
    Volume 2: Writing towards Writing and Reading:
        On Poetics, with Implicated Readings

John Hall

As a said place

Poems

First published in the United Kingdom in 2017 by
Shearsman Books
50 Westons Hill Drive
Emersons Green
BRISTOL
BS16 7DF

Shearsman Books Ltd Registered Office
30–31 St. James Place, Mangotsfield, Bristol BS16 9JB
(this address not for correspondence)

www.shearsman.com

ISBN 978-1-84861-503-8

Contents

Wrong from the middle   7

As a said place   12

changeable words / changeable worlds   17

I'm on the train   21

England from a distance   77

Salutations for Poetry (with Emily Critchley)   80

Notes and acknowledgements   85

Wrong from the middle

state of the person
address in which
a selection of
bad moments
has expunged the
good it is calm
now only just
away from where some
pasts still
quake & in
an unquiet world on
which the retired
depend others
fight it out Libya for
example but
bring it home too to
hold on or to hold
on to or to get hold of
some share in decisions
perhaps goods &
flows some divi
dend in action no
longer for this
awkward assemblage

that angles the left
over pieces to catch
a tune in the air that might
be right for the rough
times ahead what
do you do with where
you find yourself
alone faced it
seems with a choice as
between distracted
attention just
as though you were
needed saying
nothing and the awk
wardness of speaking
where there is no
reply
        wrong not
from the start
because there never
was a start in which 'you'
could have been wrong
your tiny let's imagine
pinkish white
body born into
history that is to say
in a colonised land

as though there were
any other you the
coloniser only
because that's where
you came in & at
the time didn't
know much least
of all consequences
certainly not
ambiguity in the
word 'agent' where
there was no
oil & the lure
was copper which
was here too in these
woods enough
for the employment of
say a hundred people but not
to compete with new markets
(Chile?) 'you do not
owe yourself
to the others' I said then,
'how could you?' and now
 'how could you
have said that?' but
right to have been wrong
perhaps & really

a disguised self
direction *do not*
owe your self the one
as it were accruing
capital hop
ing to live off what
is *between* (interest) and
what is to be *divided*
(dividend) and no
these aren't gods
nodding their assent your
self dizzy with numinous
debt just now
called credit be
lieve it or not you've
got to believe
to owe or can that too
be redeemed by re
versing the terms where
the literal
just won't detach
from metaphor so precisely
in debt not perhaps to
the others should they
be nameable after all that
is what a self might
be in one kind

of history the heating
oil in its bunded tank
70% up in price since the
last fill dripping
continuously 'down
fine-gauge copper tubing'
into the house for
controlled use to which
others do I owe my self
now 'it would
be foolish to regret
who we are' I said wrong
from the middle

as a said place

the negation keeps, on the soles of its shoes,
the dust of the ground it left behind (Emmanuel Levinas)

what is it
that is not
written here

                word
                touched
                body

      the world is said
      said Emmanuel Levinas

                        world
                        touched
                        bodies

          and all the bodies
          saying

in case
in the said world
there is a world
not yet said

                or one
                this one
                where the said
                is not
                quite world

everything that is the case
today

in the sung world
the figured world
the said world

imagined to be the case
said
to be imagined

sighed
signed
as desire

but not desired
to be not

no
he said
a willed minus
swells
no he said
is more than

(different at the food-table,
perhaps)

every subject's debt
to the one nearby

he who has lost his place

death is the no-response [*sans réponse*]
said Levinas

13

        the living
        cannot
        not respond

nothing to say
because I do not see your face

        or you choose
        not to see my face

           replies that are not replies
           and are thus more than replies
           the call given
           a call
           for a given
           response

tactical fakes
planted to raise the value
of the genuine

    real ladies don't buy fakes
    it says
    only the genuine

  genu, knee (*a father acknowledges*
  paternity of a new-born child
  by placing it on his knee)

   this act is
   precarious, obtained by prayer
   when the call was fear

   the one-reply of a father's body

    alternatively
    genus: birth, race, stock, kind
    either way
    a precarious call
    on authenticity

                the balance reflex
                                that stabilizes
                                                the eyes
        it is normal
                        to feel a little dizzy
                                        adjust
        your speed
                        so that the writing
                                        just
        steps
                out of focus
                                at the limit
        of tolerance
                        you could stand
                                        in front
        of a mirror or window

unusual stimulation
of the vestibular receptors and semi-circular canals also can
give rise to sensory distortions in
visual and motor activity
the resulting discord
often leads
to nausea and disorientation

        a damaged balance system has little
        ability to repair itself.

changeable words / changeable worlds

This autumn we celebrate the power of words to
change the world for the better.
(London Literature Festival, 2014)

what can poets do
whose means are words
but whose scenes of words
are not
the assemblies of the polis

should we (and who are we)
treat the words as
strictly of the household
of the privacy or even privation
of intimacy?

the scenes of the poem are more than
the poem
the poem has responded to its imagined
scenes
the poet may not
be altogether helpless in this

a political solution

that words might undo
what other words
are doing

no boots on the ground solution

the abstraction
of military violence
to a great height
or distance
much like
words

tasks for poets in times of war

silence
incitement
exhortation
abomination
appeasement
reportage
lying
membership
justification
calls on the divine
on the power of the names
of secured values

attending keenly to what it is
that words can do
to the words that can do

behaving as though
there is no war

lazy words

words is a lazy term
for what happens
when people speak and hear each other
or write and read each other
or sing to or with each other
poems are more than words

a poem cannot on its own

a poem
cannot on its own
undo history
(what might poem
be a lazy term for?)
where history
is the past
still told and lived
a scene
supposedly
telling itself

a poem may attempt
to declare its own scene
in a sleight-of-text
meant to deceive itself

a poet can hear this happen
perhaps helplessly
but how does a poem
undo its own betrayals?

between us

and who is us anyway
the sharing and divisions
of vocabulary and rhythm
are facts of politics
of the 'world'

counter-moves by poets
can distance
the very those
they are intended to help

politics must assume
the ever-potentiality
of a 'we'
but usually instead
asserts a singular plural of
we is who you say I is

this may be the space
of the poem.

coda

a single syllable
in a lyric poem

I'm on the train

1. with a view

getting on the train

          with a view

to write in

       transit

  ive

     west

wards

       already

so far west the

        east

pulls behind

      bridges

where the river

       becomes

           winding

estuary

    cutting

       what could be 'countries'

in a severance

     west

that is just now

      being argued

         north

but as for me

        I travel

to work

      which is to say

towards the body

          that pays me

2. a wholly owned subsidiary

three minutes late a change
at Plymouth that is no change the
conductor explains as she issues
an off-peak return 15.38 three coaches nearly
empty Plympton already its 'industrial' estate
a state of diligence possible
Latin root says Skeat to *build*

                                        within

which I like since industry
in the world that pays me
is nothing so abstract
as 'a state of' more a collective
name for all those who
work with exchangeable
goods at some
scale, volume or price
so the outer walls of these
buildings bound a *without* on which
apparently we all depend and that's
without in the sense of *outwith* since
it would not do to imply any lack
in all that diligent activity

                                Sept 15th

it's fine nearing the equinox
various cautions Safety Information Litter the
red cross over the lit cigarette means
Don't or Go *Without* slowing down a
complex sound change a subtle

inner body adjustment (within) those
who live near railway lines full view
of the platforms at Plymouth
check what the conductor said
against the announcement

                      'terminates here'
check the score in Gros Islet check
emails I think that is good news about
her kidneys I might lose my
leg-room school's out nearby Nash
161 not out that's in England not
Gros Islet it's loud now and there's
someone perched up across from me
on a seat that folds back Italia
a badge says on his upper
sleeve after school chocolate
cup-cake Doritos Frito-Lay a
wholly owned subsidiary
of PepsiCo she seems welcoming
of the predators how much
are they phones as well but only
two in sight his across the way and
two (that makes three now
doesn't it) clutched by uniformed girls and now
another a mother her phone in a pink
case her baby tries to thumb the icons and
is encouraged nearly time to set off
for Truro doors have closed an official
whistle a surviving technology
westwards through more
parts where people reside see
under *sedentary* says Skeat before

to the south docks is that
the Sound or the Tamar behind
buildings that must be naval
organisations or maritime at least
Devonport says it Stop
to let more on & off if I knew
how to read their badges I'd know which
schools Dockyard doors in this
carriage don't open yes there's the
water again and then
lost to view in the cutting at
Keyham this is local transport more
on at St Budeaux some of the girls
out good-bye their friends say the baby
has spotted some food on the
way it's a bribe to get strapped in seems
young to me to be eating Quavers one of the
Frito-Lay International brand names there's
the boundary river at low tide certainly the
Tamar this time moorings neatly
lined up & down stream & at some
point on the crossing it's
Cornwall Goodbye guys says
another about to alight
at Saltash and behind us now the last
'English' city

3. *Performic* **but not the acid**

21st October train delayed
what's left
of Hurricane Gonzalo eleven
minutes two emails
on the phone
to think about did I
recall a conversation
in 1974
with a now dead
and still
fine poet had I written
on a particular term
that I thought
useful though absent
from dictionaries No
and Yes but the No needs
a careful answer and the Yes
detail and a search
through computer files
and meanwhile the journey
has become no more
than NOISE as in
information theory
and literally too something
being wrapped NOISILY
in the seat behind me the
crispest paper sellotape
pulled against its own

sticky resistance I don't
look round it's loud
all right but with Noise
you have to know
what counts as Signal

4. implacable

the place I am in
                    moves
through other places
                        like the inner part
of one of those
                    slide rules are they
still used each
                    alignment
of marks contingent but
                        repeatable if
I were to say
            between places I
might mean a new
                    place
formed by the sliding
                        contiguity
of two places or it
                    might be
that I don't know
                    the names
of these fields woods roads
                            places
enough if you in
                habit them *keep them*
in you Skeat
                doesn't quite say
moving through and along
                        them in

the habitual repetitions
                    of works days and
places this
            journey that is
in my day
            has as its own
undercarriage I speak literally
                        wheels and
these on
            fixed rails sleepers
marking off
                progress
towards a selected
                    destination
in syncopation with the Zeno
                        spokes
on the wheels fixing
                    through habit
a strict
            procedure
a rhythm of the course
                        no
frivolous adventure in words
                        and thoughts as though
new to me as I circle
                    back
to the named place
                    of old
thoughts it will not be enough to
                        remember
circling
            an image of

Image steady or

        flaring in mind and

is it mind it is so

        abstract

yet bodily too this

        spectre

of concept this

        will

to see out of thought

        alone

where Keats found

        truth awoken

from the first

        dream of all

5. nights including those to come

i.

in sleep it seems

        the journeys

are mostly there

        to be delayed

and consequently

        in their turn

to cause other delay

        resistance

in every medium

        thickening

supposedly traversable space

        it's not

Hurricane Gonzalo some

        incompetence

impossible to disown

        the packing

not done not even

        thought

about tickets and passports

        in some

other house some other town

        perhaps

in that jacket carelessly

        left over a chair

recalculating all the time

        weighing up

the consequences of

        belatedness

dream-time obstacles unkindly
                        light
obscuring the way ahead
                    as when
road markings
                are nearly lost
in mist or the evening
                  rain
spreads unstoppably in
                    from the nearby Atlantic

ii.

PS Hungary a conference perhaps somewhere
in the furthest reaches dream geography
is speculative on this point and
here I am dawdling over breakfast
and other guests who are more important than
I am are in the same boat (or more to the
point not) and seem not to be bothered

iii.

it is a likeness
of nothing at all
it is a trace
before the event
of what might be thought

it abuts a space a gap
an interval
and then there is
another likeness
of nothing at all
of what might be thought
a constellation
of such likenesses
adding up to
a precarious image of images
not graven of course blink
and the outline is lost

iv.

these fields so
unlike each
other in some
respects marked
by hedges in
tessellation each
one named as is
necessary
for property and
constellation the
unlikeness
of contiguity the
likeness
of comparison and
of course there
may be a family
resemblance
between contiguous
differences the
world is only
in part
structured like
a language of
course the fields
are alike
in their
differences

6. emergency appeal

the little pamphlet by Jeremy Prynne
Al-Dente resting at a sliding angle
on a pile that includes the visible heading
Ebola Emergency Appeal and a letter from the
local MP inviting me and everyone else no doubt
in this corner of TQ11 to a meeting
that I can't get to it is
an autumn afternoon and my eyes
are heavy any effort
physical or mental is there
to be avoided I have read
the little book (Prynne) with
familiar puzzled pleasure
and even begun to trace patterns
in it that may well have been one
source of the pleasure the way they
can be with him but now looking at
it with its cover ajar through
hooded eyes how
did I ever lift its
words to my ears and eyes and
how could I ever
do so again acuity
when it is in hiding is
difficult to recall or even suppose
its recovery to be
possible on another
table to my right is a *Collected Poems*

of Emily Dickinson these
can seem at first very
simple in comparison but even so
or especially this is not the moment
to get these poems singing
far from simply the way
they can to a clear-eared
reading but who knows
writing this has perhaps
a little unhooded my eyes

7. Banquet of abstemiousness

Emily: Feminine of the Teutonic Emil, the
'industrious'
(Susan Howe, *My Emily Dickinson*)

then close the valves of attention
on mortal lips divine
and long for the long shadow
of so-called experience

as presentiments on the lawn
as rumours of delirium
as undeveloped freight
zeroing to the bone

O mortal lips divine
give me the precious gift
of darkening experience
O quality of loss

the freight
of a sacrament
candid in May
nonchalant in death

private like a breeze
qualified by loss
touching lips with mortality
in brief tragedies of flesh

§

imperceptibly as grief
summer lapses away
too nonchalant in its death
sinking with the sun

it was covert in April
as cool to speech as stone
chilling the syllables
pressed under its weight

while suns go down
and trade encroaches
private breezes
lap the summer's loss

and cool to speech like stone
imperceptibly grievous
bones at a banquet of abstemiousness
texts avoiding mourning

8. off-rail

wheeling the barrow up and slightly across the steeply
sloping field marking a path in the wet grass the intention to
head for the log-piles as nearly straight as the contours and
my own footedness allow this is tilting surface not inclined
plane in other words not straight at all this is now the Way
since each journey has its own return and the task will be
repeated with just those variations required by the positions
of the piles and the shapes of the logs when there is one
big and cylindrical enough to roll of course it has its own
contours and will not follow the Way rolling to a stop each
time at a different place altogether calling for improvisation
and new ways

9. working

working on the train
not the same as working on the trains
which unlike Lee
I have never done four minutes
late at Ivybridge the conductor's
ticket machine isn't working
in either sense a set of files
on my electronic tablet
for Saturday's meeting in
Somerset talked
briefly with someone getting out
at Plymouth about the way to Mt
Gould Hospital noticed the water
when Saltash was announced looked
out to check the platform signs
at St Germans Bodmin Lostwithiel
otherwise this sliding
and rolling place annulled
by the abstractions
of literate attention

10. quite specific

what if
> it is
>> exactly

when you have
> nothing
>> to say

that even so you
> try to say
>> that

quite
> specific
>> nothing

11. The Exchange

the first off-peak train
of the day commuting
those who must travail
on public transport between
residence and work it
will reach Plymouth
for a 9.30 start there is
no easy seat I stand
in the seatless space
where the doors are and
glance around my eye
snagging on a bearded stranger
who slowly commutes in my
distracted cognition into
recognised friend thus
crossing a border of
contraries though friends do
carry their strangeness about
with them even in their
beards and this is in part
who else they can
be after Plymouth
we sit together we both have
work to do but talk
to do as well we
manage both up to a
point the talk
arising from the two

different kinds of work that
up to a point we share the one
that pays us for today
and the one that sustains
both of us I guess through
pleasure and purpose one
has the fixed address
that is our immediate
destination the other
is a scattered map of
those who have found
each other over
distance or might yet
do so through the abstracted
outcomes of what they do and
make it is fruitless
to try to work after
Truro and we are still
talking on the walk
up to the newer campus
of a University that was once
an arts school with
those two kinds of work
supposedly combining it is blowing
hard and wet when we part
by the old library doors the new
one now part of *The*
Exchange the value
of knowledge and literate
pleasure can go down as well as up

12. in the dream

I'm in the dream and doubly so it seems the walk
is an outing rather than a journey the latter
assumed to have a destination the former having
as its purpose pleasure who knows
who these people are or why we are here together
I do know where we are since I used to live
nearby this must be a dream I tell them I know
because it is all too green and not only that
look over there where the sea should be
instead there is a flat stretch of still water
whose near shore is interrupted
with a gap like one in a reservoir-wall shaped
to control overflow perhaps here
to control flow between two different
ideas of the world though in the dream
the water seems contained in possible
defiance of the borders and passages
humans so often adapt from nature look
down there that settlement wasn't there before it's
a dream all right I say in the dream

13. stay true

rising early and dark
& leaving behind the book
that I was to have read
Paul Ashton's *The Flight Into Egypt*
in which he tells in novel form
the adventures of Jesus's family
as they flee from Herod
slipping between the detailed
naturalism that must have occasioned
hours of research & a mode in which
gods and animals can talk with the
favoured young in other words
fable rather than novel
Mary has just died from a snake bite
though unlike Cleopatra's
this was in no way planned
and my plan which was to read past
this death is stymied no
slipping into that parallel activity
that constant sliding of narrated event
narrated by others that is in
& around what does not seem as yet
narrated though its chapters are gaps
between stations whitened
with frost & it's cold in here too
especially with the doors open at
the stations at least I have on
several layers in anticipation

though the guy who got off at
St Germans seemed fine
with his arms exposed his t-shirt
& jeans marked by the particular
soil of his trade his tattoos
faded as the remembered
dreams of his youth I assume
without any right to do so
since we didn't talk

14. imperfect formation

getting on the train
             again
                   a necessary
repetition
        the train that is
                no need
to keep saying
        it
           the repetitions
of the days
        lost in
         rhythms
of speech already
          themselves
               changing
patterns of
        doing it again
             just as
the songs are there
          as it were
             in the air
hanging
      in the ear
         ready
for repeat
       performances
           and just as
most songs are
        patterns of
            repetitions
at different levels
         beginning again
             so often a way

of moving
          in place
                    in my bag
tasks for the journey
                    lined up
                              as though
there are station calls
                    between them
                                        these words
of unknown duration
                    one of the tasks
                                        of course they
differ in
          urgency
                    and lie
on an imagined
                    line
                    between
simple pleasure
                    and pained duty
                                        somewhere
on this
          sliding scale
                    even
the duty
          is pleasurable
                    a bonus
lightening
          the debt of pay
                    an item
in the prospectus
                    of tasks is
                              check
the draft reply
                    to one who has
                              some control

over my pay
              and therefore
                           over me he
wants because he is in
                  difficulties
                           to reduce
my cost to the firm
               to which end
                        he has decided
that not all my services
                are needed
                     my age
being no longer
             a legitimate pretext
                         he may find
this restraint
          difficult in turn
                    the one
who controls his pay
              has likened
                       her own leadership
to command of the
             Red Arrows in
                    perfect
V formation
           which reminds me
                   that though pay
is descended
          from a word for
                pacify
the highest
        paid
           are not conspicuously
the most peaceable
          nor most aware
                  of their debts

I am glad to say
          this is not all
                   a matter
of daily repetition
          in my case
                  or at least
not yet
      imagine
         each day
you resist
      all over again
              erosion
of your contract
        it happens or
                that's how it
feels there is
      a difference
            is there not
between
      repetition
         as patterned
figure and
      repetition
         as the how-it-is
of ground
      it is
        March 3rd
so much
      has changed so much
             is as it is
in early March

15. going nowhere

so the point of a train
is that it goes somewhere
near where you're going
and while it does so
you have a view of or through
more than one window unless
it is so crowded you can't see
past the next head you are
standing or sitting let's say sitting
and though it is the train that moves
everything that is not the train
in other words the 'world'
appears to move past
unless it is dark outside and you are
in a reflective space tubed
off from the world except
for flashes of light or
the thudding and shaking
sprocket movements as the
lit windows of a contrary
train jump in and out of
alignment in a familiar
reversal much as the terms
sunrise and *sunset* still imply
that it is the sun that rises and
'sets' and there are no single
words that I know for the earth's
daily roll into light or

darkness so I am in the train
actually on this occasion I'm
not but this present tense is
not a lie so much as a familiar
trick of social imagination getting
the sprocket holes of multiple
strips of time suitably
aligned I sit still
in my seat with a thrumming of
movement under me and in my
head I'm using what I know
of being on a train to try to
understand something let's say
that on that train I have
another 'window' the one this
time that is the screen
of my smart-phone I hold it
still in my hand but it is
full of change and movement
whether or not I look at it
it is full of designed chance
something all the time called
news which is the world
apparently and then
thrumming networks of social
imagination working at speed hey
john I keep tabs on time check
it as something still out there I
know how little of it
matters and this doesn't
matter either actually I
am at home the screens

of my computer are open to the same
proxy events as if I were
on the train some of these
people are my friends and some
of it matters they might be the bearers
of messages or they might themselves
be the messages angels in other words

16. Great Western

between Plymouth and Truro
              Chapters II to XI of Peter
Riley's *Due North* not this time
            a long poem
tracing a journey or
             quest but leaps
between different
            points in a
constellation
            that he can make
out clearly enough these
            points are
fragments of memories and
            knowledge all to him
in plain speech as
            well as view
movements
            in waves eddies
returns of melancholy elegies
            for losses recited in
hope of better a
            plurality of losses endured
by a singular
            known as *we* or *us*
or *choral I* losses
            like this lack
destination
            alas loss

being a medium through
              which
forward movement
              is constrained though
utterance of loss can
              take due bearing
within movements other
              than itself such
as in music or poems
              lamentations
or lachrymae my
              journey without tears
condensed to the pure terms
              of time as exchangeable
currency there is
              Due North anywhere
on earth except the
              North Pole Cecil
Rhodes for example
              imagined another
Great North Road all
              the way up
Africa as means and
              mark of decisive
entrepreneurial navigation
              these magnetic
terms so often
              shorthand for ethnic
and economic
              conditions I am in the
South West travelling
              in a westerly direction

through a county whose
        'economic performance
is now the worst in the UK' read
        more in the Cornish
Guardian and whose people
        enjoy recognised minority status
under the rules of the European
        Union on whose
development money
        my pay almost
certainly depends
        as I read
Due North
        on what remains
of the Great
        Western Railway

PS
what remains of
        what returns
under the name
        of the same
this grand
        hoarding
on Truro station
        We
are giving the West
        back its Great
Western Railway

17. about other things

looking up from Radnóti's poems
to see that we're crossing the bridge
again I have to make the usual
effort to get the train moving in the
right direction through careful
orientation of the map in my head set
squarely on a page with North
at the top Radnóti was in no
position to get things going in
the right direction as the dates
on the bottom of each page
show great emblems found in
poems and everyday life for
example sky sun moon rain
poignantly counter to the pain
inflicted by let's say European
history joined to verbs that unsettle
I live he says I am surprised that I live
I tried to write about other things
he wrote in another poem but
it was no use

18. mirror writing

driving east because the train
timings don't work so you know
that this isn't written in the
specified transit nor with a view
to a contemplative view other
than the road ahead that mesmerising
drone of meditation scored to the strips of
white road markings this may be
to take the way of writing very
literally a scriptive movement of a hand
over a page say or fingers softly
touching keys so much of it starts
up as a strip of language sounds
in the head and only poor memory
says to write it down but you can't
easily behind the wheel unless it's
safe and legal to do so make
an effort at phonic memory which
may already be writing first turn
the radio off the sound world transfers
frictional rhythm metallic and rubberised
already passed through various
absorbers the slightest vibration through

seat and wheel at too rapid

a frequency even for phonemes though

not for voicing the Cornish road swaying

and dipping the way ahead coming in

and out of view no stations on a two-hour

journey apart from road works and other

frustrations familiar waymarks instead

where the logic of the route plays

itself out the destination event

as well as place seized

in advance in a set of moves

called preparation an anticipated

number on the tripmeter retrospection

expected in the east later the

driving mirror perched high and as

though interrupting the windscreen an

early model perhaps of a window in

a window these devices for keeping

the wind out while looking

from an *in* to an *out* and especially

perhaps from an *in* to an *in*

19. on the look-out

on at Ivybridge again on
      the look-out this time
            for a ten-syllable line
to swap with Peter (Hughes)
      but it is the busy train
            and the one seat available
is in the middle of a row of three
      itself a line of a kind though
            in this arrangement one
line does not lead to another so
      much as correspond to it without
            resemblance to melodic
sequence or sentence
      structure except
            possibly for the conductor
making his way down the rows
      checking and selling tickets it's
            too awkward to reach for a pad and
pen so in my ear I try out
      a few ten-syllable lines
            whose theme
anticipates the bridge over the Tamar
      the expanded
            early middle so to speak
of this repeated journey slow and
      in its perspectival depth sumptuous
            up and down river and each
time different not
      least because
            anticipation itself varies for
example it is precisely
      Brunel's bridge I see in advance
            with its place in

engineering history not to
        mention tourist guides but
                when I am actually on it I
don't see *it* at all because I see
        from it like looking out
                of my own face whereas
from the road bridge
        alongside it anyone
                can read BRUNEL
and 1859 too as the year
        when the bridge and
                his life were
both completed
        and the single noun ENGINEER
                not a verb in sight perhaps
monuments are what happens
        when verbs become nouns
                there is no
other bridge quite like this I say
        as though I knew
                more about bridges
than any *this*
        bridge (or *that* bridge)
                and could survey in my
head all bridges
        actually built let
                alone imaginable
all effortlessly suspended
        in the word 'bridge'
                as determined more by
function than instance and
        transcending proper names *this*
                is the Royal Albert
Bridge as I write
        Peter is probably in Hebden Bridge
                rather than on it that's a place

named after its bridge while *this* bridge
           that I haven't reached yet except
                in anticipation joins
two named places and enacts a union
           of continued separation see how the acts
                of association that link two
sides of meaning cannot be
           held back from a word like *bridge* and
                meanwhile it is Plymouth and there's
Mark the ten-syllable lines
           are displaced
                by the different impulsions of talk

20.   return tickets

late June
  the busy train is
    less busy today as
      far as Plymouth but
        picks up a little
        after that it's
        the kind of day
        for an outing
      if you have
    the time that rucksack
for example
 is for walking she sits
   tranquilly with it
     on her lap and talks
       to no one though the woman
         next to her
           might be her silent
           companion my head
         has been down over a
       laptop too big
     for the gap between the
rows I have barely looked
up even at stops I have a
  draft to read of some chapters
    that are full of interest to me
      and part of my job is to
        help with them he writes
          about artists who walk or
          set walking tasks
        for others the walks

he describes cannot
easily be called
migrations
especially in the light
of current news that
has made migration
a fearful term
for some and that fear
politically useful
for others many
of these migrations
in the news are undertaken
at extreme risk of life or in
carceration in hope
of another life in this
carriage there seems
a tranquil sense
of entitlement to travel
without risk the migrants
in the news are unlikely
to head for Cornwall
if they are at all
informed

21. this could be the last time
Lee Harwood (6 June 1939 – 26 July 2015)

shall I call this the last journey of the
    year or will that be the next one it
certainly isn't the first though I am
    back from holiday and holidays
are intended to divide the year into
    stops and starts I am looking for
good endings in one or two
    aspects of my life and this may have
something to do with Lee's death
    last week well before his time a man
of clear lyrical pleasures still
    attentive to the detailed movement and
stillness of a world that answered
    his own like those shuddering frames
when two trains pass each other we
    never actually travelled down to
Cornwall together though we
    met up at St Ives with
Melanie and Kelvin for the
    Hilton exhibition and he did
join us at Birdie and Susie's wedding
    in Treyarnon where we slept
one above the other in the
    youth hostel bunks and
he gave me the benefit of his
    knowledge as a theatre
dresser respecting always the

skilled particularities of work
with no sense at all that his
    poet's calling put him
above all that or that there is a
    life of the mind somehow preferable
to the knowledgeable
    labours of the skilled here
it is the holiday season the train
    is fuller than it usually is after
Plymouth Lee's eyes would be
    quietly at work inside and
out especially over the water
    the windows marking both
beginning and end his ear
    hearing the lyrical traces of the
speech around us though right
    now that is mostly
muffled by all the sounds
    that the train makes

22. an end of sorts, a return

travelling eastwards

        this time

                on what my ticket

calls a return

      picking up

            what used to be

the Intercity

      at Par

          on its holiday route

from Newquay hardly

        a city I'm earlier

              than usual and

the day has given me much

        to think about

             the body

that pays me

      will not be doing so

           for much longer

it has ideas for its future

       the way bodies with CEOs

             tend to

that require a different if

       in some respects

           imaginary

cast list of payees

      I am invited to

          consider

expressing my interest

       in severance

          since my post will be

deleted following full review

      and restructure

          the invitation

is in its way

        compelling

                these journeys

like so many

        are contingent

                and they will

stop

23. first tail, without disparagement

well here I am on another
            return journey
with no sense that anything
            new has started
rather that
            things are failing
to end well and that
            the willed simplicity
of that monosyllabic
            STOP
has exercised no magic
            powers
on others has done
            no more than mime I
allude to J L Austin
            an infelicitous
gesture of termination
            since few of the
conditions for felicity
            were in place in
journeys from a to b
            b is seldom truly
conclusive in the larger
            scheme of things it is no
more than a hop-off point
            in one of those city
subway systems London
            or Glasgow for

example where each journey
            is an individual arc
cut from the train's
            obsessive circling the one
tactical the other
            strategic as with
Brunel's bridge it
            all depends
where you see it
            from
and whether you are one of those
            who can see
circle and arc at once
            like that trick
of patting
            your head
with one hand while
            rubbing your stomach
in circles with the other
            the temporal
arts and rites
            may all have
something to do with this
            of course everything else
goes on but just for now
            let's call this
a beginning which
            has been arranged
by those in strategic
            command of
starts and stops
            there are these faults

in time where it can be
       bent at angles
or snapped in
       two leaving gaps
across which any
       remaining charge
must arc leading often
       to unexpected
consequences

23. second tail, lifting: Xs in flight from algebra

(a variation on two lines from Emily Critchley)

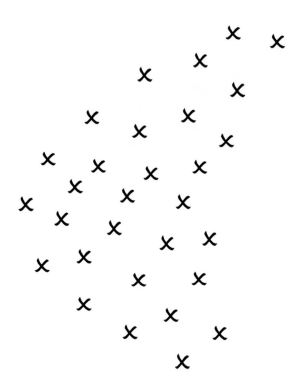

15.9.2014 - 5.10.2015

England from a distance

bind the soil with thinned molasses
pack it down and roll it to a smoothness
stretch a tight coir mat over its twenty-two yards
peg it down nothing
to inspect except tautness

home is obviously a county
probably one prominent in Wisden
Surrey for example winning everything
and being quite different from London
whereas Yorkshire is mysterious
and not a country to claim
lightly as your own be respectful
but wary the *gentlemen* are more likely
to be batsmen and captains of course
playing without wages because they
have the means among the bowlers
there is a distinction
between speed and guile the one
requiring stature and athleticism
the other allowing for less than
athletic deviousness this is
of course different for the captain whose
cleverness is natural to him

     keep your head still and your eye
     on the ball at times you might need
     to hit your way out of trouble anything
     will do as a bat so long as you can
     hold it upright and swing it in a clear

arc from a sideways-on stance there must be
a part of it acting as handle and part as blade any
kind of ball will do though this will depend
on what you are using as a bat

shave the paint carefully
off each plane on the end of
a hexagonal pencil and mark
the flats at least as follows: 0, 1, 2, 4, 6, W
name your team after your friends
or the Test team or maybe the
1957 Surrey XI there must be
eleven because this is a mystical
prime number relating to the average size
of a cricket field it would be inappropriate
to make the names up though this has been done
by writers of course the probabilities
are quite different from those of a live game
though either can offer intense
numerological pleasure the game
can lead to results of kinds
including a no-result in which
the real opponent may be time itself
or time's proxies weather and light

the game is always open
to assessments of technique imagination
and grace since recital of the score
is barely adequate indeed
there is a special mode
of synchronised narrative and another
of retrospective prose
for which the score is no more
than context this prose

is itself open to aesthetic judgement even
so keep the score meticulously do
the averages you are supposed
to play for the team not your average but
do the sums to two decimal points

base your field placings on the diagram
in Patsy Hendren's book later
you might learn the guile of tactical
placements change the bowling by
formula until you understand
what you are doing if you
are still batting at the end of play
keep going tomorrow it is
very unfortunate to get out at 49 you will
remember the disappointment
for a long time being 'out'
can bring instant and irreversible
sense of failure and error if not
shame when bowling you
must finish the over even
when you are being humiliated

the ball is far too small
to be seen clearly from the boundary
to enjoy watching you must
interpret from a distance
and this requires trained knowledge whereas
on TV now they will show the stitching
and then show it all over again

the grass must be as level and even as possible
do not take the work of the ground staff for granted

Salutation to Poetry

with Emily Critchley, and for Claire Tredgett

The advanced silence:
>   *overwhelmed by speech*
>   *that holds back*

The book of the breast:
>   *as one in rhythm*
>   *needing breath*

The non-immediate immediate:
>   *that interrupts*
>   *that doesn't interrupt*

The trans-temporal friendship:
>   *across how many times*
>   *how many times*

The anti-capitalist cry:
>   *making manifest through sounds*
>   *that mark absence*

The non-materialist material:
>   *the breath, the thinnest veil of ink*
>   *shadows against a screen*

The ghost in the machine:
>   *a spectral voice that doesn't speak*
>   *that speaks otherwise*

The yogic exhalation:
out
breath

The necessary differance:
speaking
to no one

The company in a crowd:
o my songs
lost

The work that no one paid or even asked for:
unknown debt
obliquely honoured

The spiritually semantic:
aspirate, dispirited
sighing with meaning and its loss

The gunman's heart:
lowered toward your breast-book

The unacknowledged guest:
come in
out of that happy cause

The imagined voice erotic:
where does that si
-lence tend?

The movement of desires that have lost their bodies
    in other arrows

The politics of the unsaid:
    to speak being
    to misrepresent

That doesn't know what it knows:
    in other moves

That moves to the movements of others' tongues:
    Refraining from the world
    if you can

That replies to a missing question:
    in
    breath

That is imperilled by the silence of pages:
    [   ]

That speaks as though it sees your face:
    So hum

That is hot though mute in the ear:
    coming urgently
    to meet you

That is neither speech nor song though both:
    adding up to almost everything

Acknowledgements and Notes

Wrong from the Middle was first published in *Snow lit rev 2*, edited by Anthony Barnett and Ian Brinton.

The title poem, **As a said world**, was included in a celebratory collection assembled by Matt ffytche for Andrea Brady's birthday.

changeable words / changeable worlds is included in *A Festschrift for Tony Frazer,* edited by Richard Berengarten, Martin Anderson, Kelvin Corcoran, Lucy Hamilton, Aidan Semmens and Lynda Waters (*http://tonyfrazer.weebly.com/*).

The poems that make up **I'm on the train** were written between 15th September 2014 and 5th October 2015 in the order in which they appear here. With the exception of a PS added later to poem 16, 'Great Western', I have not attempted to update allusions to topical matters. This applies particularly to poem 20, 'Return tickets'.

England from the distance was written for and is included in *Leg Avant: the new poetry of cricket* (Crater 35), edited by R.T.A Parker.

A Salutation to Poetry was written collaboratively with Emily Critchley and produced as a letter-pressed broadsheet (Crater 32) by Richard Parker. My thanks to Emily for her permission to include the poem here.

My thanks to the editors named above